These 'manners for the multitude'
were first published in 1907.

NEVER

NEVER COMPLAIN, NEVER EXPLAIN, NEVER DO ANYTHING ECCENTRIC

By Walter Emanuel

"Well I Never!" ~ Popular Confession

Copper Beech Publishing

Published in Great Britain by
Copper Beech Publishing Ltd
©Copper Beech Publishing 1997

All rights reserved.
Without limiting the rights reserved under copyright above, no part of this publication may be reproduced, stored in or introduced into a retrieval system or transmitted in any form or by any means without the prior written consent of the publisher.

ISBN 978 1 898617 25 9

A CIP catalogue record for this book is available from the British Library.

Originally published in London by Sir Isaac Pitman and Sons Ltd.

Copper Beech Publishing
PO Box 159 East Grinstead
Sussex England RH19 4HF
www.copperbeechpublishing.co.uk

NEVER!

PREFACE

One frequently reads of a man, "He has an imposing manner." But in my opinion, a man should have more than one manner. Hence this handbook - which, it is hoped, may result in our becoming a Nation of Gentlemen.

What is a gentleman? The best definition, perhaps, is: A gentleman is one who has a certain something about him which is quite indefinable. I met one at a dinner-party some twelve months ago.

NEVER

When a clumsy waiter spilled a plateful of thick mock turtle down his back, all he said was, "I asked for clear soup."

That was a gentleman! Pretty manners, it should never be forgotten, go a long way.

Nothing, in fact, is ever lost by being polite except the reputation of being a boor. I feel that no further excuse for this book is needed.
W.E.

NEVER

Gentlefolk are always nice to their servants.

THE TREATMENT OF SERVANTS

Gentlefolk are always nice to their servants.

◦⌒◇⌒◦

Never call servants '*Servants*'.

'*Paid Guests*' is the expression least calculated to give offence.

◦⌒◇⌒◦

Never carry on a conversation in a foreign language before servants. It is calculated to hurt their feelings. Besides which, in these days of universal education, they may understand what you are saying. Still, it will be fairly safe for the average Englishman to make a confidential remark in French before the French maid.

NEVER

Never chide a servant in the presence of strangers. Remember that she cannot answer back and if she does, you may feel sorry.

◈

In addressing servants never omit the usual little politenesses. They expect them. Take the following conversation:-

Master:- "Oh, will you get me my boots?"
Maid:- "If what?"
Master:- "Oh, if you please?"
Maid:- "If you please what?"
Master:- "Will you kindly get me my boots, if you please, Miss?"
Maid:- "That's better. No, I won't."

NEVER

Remember that she cannot answer back ...

NEVER

Never try to alight from a lady's train when in motion.

DINNER PARTIES

Never ask a friend to dine with you "in quite a friendly way." It insinuates that he usually quarrels when he dines with you.

∽

If you are a bachelor, and are invited to dinner at a house where there are a number of spinster daughters, never be so coarse as to reply that you regret to say that you are not a marrying man.

∽

Never try to alight from a lady's train when in motion.

NEVER

Nor is it good form to refuse an invitation, even if you have been to the house before, on the ground that you are going to have a headache that evening!

◊

Never arrive at a dinner-party before the hour mentioned on the invitation. If this should happen, owing to your cabby having driven quickly, a capital way of passing the ten minutes or so which you have to spare is to underpay the cabby. By the time you have finished the fight you will be able with decency to enter the house.

◊

If, however, you are a weakling, and the cabby is a modern Samson, overpay him, and enter at once. Explain to your host and hostess,

NEVER

A capital way of spending the ten minutes you have to spare is to underpay the cabby.

– who come flying down to receive you, that you know you are too early, that they need not speak to you for ten minutes, and beg your host to go upstairs again and put on his tie, and point out to your hostess that, owing to her maid's carelessness, one of her cheeks is enjoying ruddier health than the other.

Never arrive late at a dinner-party. If you do, try and think of a better excuse than "Sorry, but I was not hungry."

NEVER

However dull a dinner-party may be, never produce a book from your pocket, prop it up against a candlestick, and begin reading it - even though this may lead to you never being asked to that house again.

෴

If a fish-bone sticks in your throat at dinner, on no account make a fuss. Quietly ask for a cat. When she is brought to you, open your mouth as wide as possible, and let puss insert her head and body, and she will soon fetch out the obstruction. Care should be taken to keep a firm hold of the hind legs, as the entire disappearance of the cat may lead to a fit of coughing, and no gentleman draws attention to himself.

෴

Never laugh with your mouth full.

If, when you are breaking up a piece of crisp jam tart, a portion flies on to the satin dress of the lady next to you, it will be best not to claim it. She might think you greedy.

༄༅

In eating cherries, do not remove the stones from your mouth and place them on the rim of your plate. The genteel thing to do is to swallow them.

NEVER

If your host, in an excess of hospitality, has pressed more wine on you than you should have taken, and you become aware of this fact on entering the drawing-room, do not try to walk, as your lurching may frighten the ladies. At once lie down on the floor, and call a hansom.

Never, after you have said "Good-bye" to your host and hostess, suddenly re-appear in the drawing room, in your overcoat, and say
"How d'you do? I am so glad to see you," and, on being pressed for an explanation, state that, to save time, you thought you would pay your after-dinner call at once, and so get it over.

NEVER

Remember that what might be looked on as smart in America may be considered eccentric in England.

○───○

Do not omit to take away a menu with you. It may help the Coroner.

○───○

NEVER

"How d'you do. I am so glad to see you."

NEVER

Fashions change.
Formerly it was the thing for men to look
very bored at Dances.
Now they need look only rather bored.

DANCES

If you are invited to a Fancy Dress Ball, never go on the wrong evening. The most correct costume is apt to look over-done then.

Never forget that fashions change from day to day. Formerly it was the thing for men to look very bored at dances. Now they need look only rather bored.

And men may dance a little at dances now.

If you should find it advisable to turn up your trousers on your way to a dance, never continue the precaution when you arrive there as your hostess may take it as a reflection on the cleanliness of her floor.

Also, if you wear a "chest-protector" to keep your shirt-front from getting soiled, remove it before entering the ball-room, unless your reputation as a humorist is firmly established.

NEVER

Remove it before entering the ball-room,
unless your reputation as a humorist
is firmly established …

NEVER

Never let the girl whom you take down to supper guess that the reason you chose her is that her beauty is not so disturbingly dazzling as to interfere with the enjoyment of your repast.

When you have sat out eight consecutive dances with the same girl never omit to tell her that the reason you do not propose to her is that you are already engaged to another girl, and that, that reminds you, you must go and see what the little flirt is up to.

NEVER

If you do propose to a girl and she rejects you with scorn, say that it really does not matter as you only did it for a bet.

Never ask a girl suddenly, "Do you paint?", or you may receive the answer, "Yes, but I did not know that it was noticeable."

༺❀༻

Never forget that if, while you are dancing, one of your partner's curls falls to the ground, you must pretend that you think it is part of your moustache - or, if you are clean-shaven, that it *is* your moustache.

NEVER

LEVÉES

On being presented for the first time, never stop and have a chat with the King. His Majesty, it is true, has a great reputation for geniality, but there is such a thing as tempting providence.

༄

Also, do not fall over your sword.

NEVER

And, if you do, and the sword breaks, do not stay to pick up the pieces. It looks grasping. Pick yourself up, and walk boldly out as though what happened was an everyday occurrence.

NEVER

NEVER

*It is quite good form to stare rudely
at members of the audience through
your opera glasses.*

AT THE OPERA

If the people on the stage persist in speaking while you are talking, never get angry with them. Remember that they are mostly foreigners, whose manners are notoriously backward.

※

It is quite good form to stare rudely at members of the audience through your opera glasses.

※

If while, from your box, you are sweeping the house with your glasses, they happen to alight on the gallery, and a rude fellow makes a long nose at you, remember that he probably cannot afford to buy a book of etiquette! On no account retort in a similar manner. The glasses, however, should be washed with a powerful disinfectant when you reach home.

If you are in the stalls, and you see a friend in the gallery, do not carry on a conversation with him from your seat - even in the interval. It is bad manners to listen to other people's conversations, and the rest of the well-bred audience would be placed in an awkward position.

NEVER

If you are in the front row of the dress circle and let your opera glasses fall, and they hit an old gentleman in the stalls, do not draw attention to the fact by making a fuss. He will do that. It is often inadvisable even to claim the glasses, for some old gentlemen are very easily upset.

Never do anything eccentric. Even if in the afternoon you have been to the Zoo, do not throw buns to the inmates of the boxes. It may be kindly, but it is bad form.

NEVER

Practise this ... as some horses, while the rider is taking off his hat, will, with innate politeness, take off the rider.

IN THE STREET

If a lady drops her purse, not only pick it up, but return it to her.

∞

Always raise your hat when you meet a lady. This must be done even though you be riding. If you are a beginner, practise this before you appear in public, as some horses, while the rider is taking off his hat, will, with innate politeness, take off the rider.

∞

If your hat has blown off, and you meet a lady, you must ask her kindly to wait till you have recovered your hat, so that you may raise it. If, however, you are wearing a wig, honour will be satisfied if you raise that.

NEVER

If, by accident, you knock up against a British Workman, and he asks you threateningly who you are "a-shoving of," do not lose your temper but answer politely (if you are of good physique), "One of the dirtiest and ugliest men I have seen for many a day."

NEVER

When a motor-car has knocked you down and passed over you, if you are feeling well enough, apologise for getting in the way and express the hope that the jolting you caused did not upset the fair occupants of the car.

Never wear motor-goggles when riding on a motor-bus. It is considered pretentious.

If, while crossing the road, you step on a banana skin, and sit down, and a number of people collect, kiss your hand to the crowd and pretend you have only done what you intended to do.

NEVER

On slapping the wrong man on the back, say to the face crimson with rage which confronts you, "Deary me, now that's funny; do you know, I took you for that scamp so-and-so!"

When, because you have paid your cabby the correct fare, he asks you, "Call yourself a gentleman?" do not argue the point, but say quietly, "No, Sir, you are my idea of a beau seigneur sans peur et sans reproche."

NEVER

If while you are walking in a deserted street, two ruffians rush up to you and ask you angrily for your money or your life, try the effect of a soft answer. Say, "Gentlemen, I should not care to give you such a worthless thing as my life, and, as regards money, I never bestow charity indiscriminately, and I must refer you to the Charity Organisation Society." Then run off swiftly.

If a beggar stops you in a fashionable thoroughfare, and asks you for a penny, give it him without more ado rather than offer to lend it him, or, while you are haggling about the rate of interest, a crowd may collect.

NEVER

When arrested in the street owing to that little matter of the forged signature on the cheque having been discovered, brazen the thing out. When your arm is linked in the constable's, walk along briskly, saying in a loud voice to the constable, "Now, you've got to come along with me to the police-station, and it will be better for you, sir, if you don't resist."

***

If a man treads on your toe by accident in the street, and says "I beg your pardon," never reply "Granted." If you wish to be thought a gentleman, scowl, and pass on without a word.

NEVER

Remember that the barber is armed with a razor.

MISCELLANEA

A gentleman should never allow a lady to pay for anything. There are fewer gentlemen among husbands than in any other class.

◈

Never draw attention to yourself. Especially if you be a pick-pocket.

◈

If a barber, while shaving you, gives you a nasty cut, never cry "..............................!" Remember that the barber is armed with a razor, while you are defenceless. Never say more than "......!"

NEVER

Do not shut your eyes when you kiss your wife's mother. It is not manly.

NEVER

◦⚭◦

Never let a lady feel embarrassed. If there is a fire at your hotel, and, in making for the escape, you meet a lady in scanty attire, remark airily, "Hot enough for one's summer things, isn't it?"

◦⚭◦

NEVER

Never address a Prince whom you meet in Society as "Your Royal Highness." Or, if you must do so, be sure to remember that the expression is "Your Royal Highness" and not "Your Royal 'Ighness."

If a peer is dining with you, do not address him as "*My* Lord," or the other guests may think he is the only one you have.

When a friend says, "How do you do?" to you, remember that it is the height of bad manners to imagine that he really wants to know, and to tell you. In any event, do not say, "Nicely, thank you."

NEVER

Nouveaux arrivés would do well to remember, in sending out invitations to an At Home, that, in the opinion of some persons, it is pretentious to announce that the hostess will "hold a Drawing-room" on the date in question.

⚜

Never make it difficult for others to be polite to you. For instance, to enter the dining-room of the most expensive room of the most expensive hotel in town, and to ask a waiter to bring you a piece of bread, a glass of water with the chill off, and a toothpick, and to look sharp about it, is not calculated to bring out the better side of the waiter.

⚜

NEVER

Be neighbourly. If a dead cat be discovered in your garden, throw it back over the wall. If you get a letter from the next-door people denying that the puss was theirs, write a polite note saying that they may keep it all the same.

Never betray excitement: remember that a parade of feelings is shockingly bad form. Nothing shows the gentleman so much as this.

NEVER

And, when the next-door people complain of your dog barking all night, do not lose your temper. Point out to them that you have never objected to their daughters singing all day.

NEVER

A nobleman who went on a hunting expedition to Central Africa, although there was not other human being within ear-shot, merely said, "Now, there's a nuisance!" when he was being eaten by a lion.

NEVER

If you are an author, and a wealthy friend suggests that you should give him a copy of your new novel, do not be so ill-mannered as to hand him six shillings, explaining that you will not be passing a shop yourself.

If an author worries you to buy his book, never be so coarse as to ask him how much royalty he gets on each copy, and when he answers, "Sixpence," give him that sum, pointing out that he will now be satisfied and you will be saved five shillings and sixpence and the trouble of reading the book!

NEVER

Vocalists also have a right to a certain amount of consideration, and, if a gifted amateur asks you to come and hear her sing, never refuse on the ground that you are musical.

◦⌒⌒◦

Remember that even artists have their feeling, and, when a talented young painter of the modern school meets you in a gallery and, pointing to a certain picture, says "I painted that," never ask him "Why?"

◦⌒⌒◦

If a friend gives you a ticket to see his play, it is bad form, when you are there, to applaud vociferously. On the other hand, you need not carry your impartiality so far as to hiss.

NEVER

Upon being shown twins, never stare at them and remark "Well, they might have been triplets."

And, if you are asked if you would like to handle one of them, never hold it up by the loose skin at the back of its neck, as this hurts the feelings of some parents.

And, upon being asked, "Don't you think they are like their father?" never answer, "Still, I daresay they will alter."

NEVER

Never hold it up by the loose skin at the back of its neck.

NEVER

When, on paying a call, you are informed by the maid that her mistress is not at home, suppress your smile of satisfaction as
   (1) the maid might tell on you,
   (2) her mistress might see you from behind the curtain.

∾

If, on leaving an At Home, you have just claimed a valuable fur coat, and the owner protests, on no account make a scene. Explain that the resemblance between his great fur coat and your shabby little light brown covert coat is astonishing.

∾

Never betray annoyance at a visitor arriving at an inconvenient hour. Be polite even to a midnight visitor. Hurry downstairs on

NEVER

hearing him arrive, ask him to excuse your not being properly dressed, explain that you did not expect him just then, and, upon his offering, in these circumstances to come again at a more convenient time, beg him anyhow to stay until you have fetched a policeman.

If, on the other hand, you are a burglar, and, while in a strange house, a dog who lives there fastens his teeth into you, and the master of the house makes his appearance, do not abuse him, but say, "If you please, sir, I've found your dog. Will you take him?"

NEVER

If you are the driver of a motor-omnibus, and you pass a horse-omnibus, sympathise with the driver, rather than jeer at him. Try some such remark as "Poor old fellow!"

※

If you are out after the birds, and you shoot your host dead, always be the first to cry, "My fault!"

Never speak without thinking. If you are playing cards, and your *vis-à-vis* says, "You are a sharp man," do not retort, "And you are a sharper, sir," without counting the cost.

NEVER

If you are a golfer, and meet with bad luck, say "Deary, deary me!"

If you do a friend a favour and he says "I am extremely grateful to you," never say "Not at all," for that would be rude. Pretend you believe him.

NEVER

Upon receipt of a mean present from a millionaire, be careful how you word your reply. Say that it is very good of him to have sent anything, and that you value his gift for the kindly thought which prompted it.

◈

When you are taken to Vine Street for being drunk and disorderly, and are asked your occupation, remember that the right expression is "Retired gentleman."

NEVER

However much you may dislike wasps,
never kill one when you see it on
a bald head without first obtaining
the permission of the owner
of the bald head.

NEVER

ETIQUETTE FOR COFFEE LOVERS
Fresh coffee - the best welcome in the world!
Enjoy the story of coffee drinking,
coffee etiquette and recipes.

ETIQUETTE FOR CHOCOLATE LOVERS
Temptation through the years.
A special treat for all Chocolate Lovers.

THE ETIQUETTE OF NAMING THE BABY
A good name keeps its lustre in the dark.
Old English Proverb

THE ETIQUETTE OF AN ENGLISH TEA
How to serve a perfect English afternoon tea;
traditions, superstitions, recipes and how to read
your fortune in the tea-leaves afterwards.

THE ETIQUETTE OF ENGLISH PUDDINGS
Traditional recipes for good old-fashioned
puddings - together with etiquette
notes for serving!

ETIQUETTE FOR GENTLEMEN
*'If you have occasion to use your handkerchief
do so as noiselessly as possible.'*

NEVER

ETIQUETTE FOR THE WELL-DRESSED MAN
Refer to this timeless advice when first impressions matter.
'Only millionaires and tramps can afford to dress badly!'

ENGLISH LAVENDER
Restore the spirits and calm the mind. Lavender is evocative of country gardens and days when life was lived at a slower pace.

RECIPES FOR GARDENERS
Garden lovers will enjoy these traditional 'recipes' and trusted hints. This book contains advice no gardener will want to be without.

RECIPES FOR ROSES
Scented bags to lay with linen, an excellent water for the head; recipes for pot pourri and sweet-smelling rose water.

For your free catalogue, write to

Copper Beech Publishing Ltd
P O Box 159 East Grinstead Sussex England
RH19 4FS

NEVER

www.copperbeechpublishing.co.uk